The Hair Extension Book

A comprehensive introduction to

hair extensions,installation and removal.

Foreword

If I could guess, you're here because you are creative, you are passionate about hair ,and you want to know everything that you can about hair extensions. You want to transform your clients in a unique way. A way,unfortunately that is not emphasized in standard cosmetology courses. You want to become knowledgeable about hair extensions in order to diversify your income. No matter your reason, you've come to the right place, because knowledge is power.

Table of Contents

Chapter 1

*Will people know it's not
mine ?*

Maybe, but there is absolutely no shame. You are free to express yourself through hair extensions. If your transformation is subtle, not many will know. If your transformation is grand, yes , people will know. So what. I mean, can I talk to you like we are sisters? The girls in my circle say, I paid for it, therefore it's

mine. You can tell people you're wearing extensions if you want, or keep it private. It's your business alone to disclose. And if no one ever told you, people do need permission to touch your hair. I'll get into "personal space" in another book.

Overall, a good installation makes sure that none of the attachments are visible. This makes for curiosity but the inability to really discern if extensions are installed and where they are. Everything should be virtually camouflaged at the scalp and throughout the hair. If this assessment meets your standards, you're good to go.

Chapter 2

Kinds of Hair Extensions

Human Hair

Human hair is usually the more expensive and highest quality of all the kinds you can purchase. Human hair comes from a person that has donated hair from their own head for one reason or another. Human hair in the form of hair pieces lasts much longer than synthetic and master mix hair. Human hair comes in a variety of textures,lengths and colors Human hair can handle the high heat of a blow dryer or flat iron and will not melt.Human hair can be chemically treated to alter the appearance and texture of it. Human hair may tangle or shed but ultimately lasts for a very long time if you take very good care of it.

1. You can shampoo, condition and detangle human hair.

2.   It can easily be styled anyway you like.

3.   You can use products specific to the hair type that you have purchased so that it will last and be easier to maintain. For example, you can use hydrating shampoos on hair that is dry, curl creams on curly hair extensions and detangler on hair that tangles.

4.   Hair extensions are not living ,so you do not need to take special care with the use of hair growth regimens and serums.They can not grow.

5.   Once you cut it, as stated earlier, it will not grow back. If you cut it but are not satisfied with the length,you will need to start over with more hair at the length it was before it was cut.

6.   It is like hair growing from your scalp in that it can be over processed by chemicals and ruined. Beware of overprocessing.

Synthetic Hair

Synthetic hair is factory made. Synthetic hair is very beautiful and silky at its appearance and the colors from dark to light are very vivid. It has never come from a human scalp. It is the cheapest hair you can buy. Synthetic hair is not designed to last for months or years.

However, with some savvy on your end, you can get it to last longer than it should. Synthetic hair can not stand up to high heat,and in general the use of heat is advised against. High heat will melt and burn synthetic hair as if it were plastic.

1. It is not human hair and cannot be handled the same way.

2. It is not expensive and is sold in many forms like ponytails,wigs and used for braids.

3. No product is needed on the hair besides a light shine spray for it to look healthy after it starts looking dull.

4. Do not sleep in this hair if it is a wig. Synthetic hair tangles easily and can be a challenge to restore to tangle free

5. No rigorous brushing and combing is needed for this hair.It is usually pre styled and cut. Brushing and combing will cause the hair to tangle up.

6. You can restore a synthetic wig with gentle shampoo and careful detangling. Air dry and a roller set if needed. Results vary.

Synthetic Mastermix

Synthetic mastermix is a combination of synthetic and human hair. The synthetic hair used in this combo is a bit stronger and can stand up to heat along with the human hair. It also is very beautiful in appearance. It comes in different lengths and colors and can be integrated for wig making, ponytail wearing or braiding hair as well.

What you should know:

1. Can be brushed,combed and easily detangled.

2. Can use heat as recommended by the vendor.

3. Comes in a variety or lengths ,textures and colors.

4. More expensive than synthetic hair alone,but less expensive than human hair.

5. Lasts longer than a regular synthetic hair piece.

6.   It is okay to shampoo gently and let air dry.

7.Styling other than its pre set style can be difficult if in wig form.

Chapter 3

Hair Insecurities

Everyone has them. The way to beat them first is with a proper client consultation. Stylists go in and have a look at the hair and scalp, growth pattern etcetera ,while we listen to you tell us what look you want to achieve. This helps us to determine if what you want is possible based on the hair you already have. Here's a bit of encouragement for anyone struggling with wanting the perfect hair(or any hair at all). Look into lace wigs. Game changer.

For everyone. Life changer. For everyone. Mood changer. For everyone. Okay, with that introduction, let's get right into the lace wigs.

Chapter 4 Lace Wigs

What is a lace wig?

A lace wig is a wig with a base made of lace. The lace is a fine thin material with grids throughout it. Single strands of human or synthetic hair are then individually tied by hand onto the grids in a pattern so that the overall look is that of a natural head of hair. A lace wig can be a full lace wig in that there is lace from fringe to nape. There are no tracks or changes in the material used to make the base of the wig. These wigs are usually expensive and last for over a year.

A lace wig can be a lace frontal wig where lace is the foundation of the front of the wig, and a different material is used for the middle and rear portion of the wig to complete the unit. Bundles of hair on wefted stacks are then sewn into the middle and rear. These are less

expensive,and can be made at home, and can last up to a year as well.

Both types of wigs can be applied with a tacky hair spray for easy removal or with adhesive,to allow you to wear it for up to a week or longer.

The lace is usually flesh toned and can be tinted to achieve your own skin color if needed.

Some lace is transparent inorder that cannot be distinguished from your skin. It

lays over your skin and "melts" or disappears.

Lace stays in place by using a tacky hair spray that allows you to remove the wig the same day . For longer wear, one can apply lace bond to the hairline, and it will remain in place for about a week or longer.

1. Most wigs offer versatility.
2. Can be shampooed and styled with heat.
3. Last months to years.
4. Lace has to be treated gently.
5. Hair spray is easier to clean from lace than lace glue/bond.

Other kinds of lace pieces

Other kinds of lace pieces include the lace frontal and the lace closure. These are human hair pieces designed to do different things. I will talk a little about each to give you a general idea of their purpose.

The lace frontal is a lace hairpiece similar to what we discussed with the lace wig. This piece is not a wig because it does not cover the whole head. This piece of hair covers about 25% of the head,however some are made to be larger to cover over half one's head if desired. They are usually 12 inches in length across the hairline and anywhere from 3-6 inches back toward the center of the head. The wider it is from fringe to the center of one's head or to the nape, the more versatile the hairpiece will be when it comes to styling.

The lace frontal hair piece can be added to a sew in,or a wig. This lace piece is to be laid about an inch in front of one's natural hairline from ear to ear to ear,like a headband. This piece is recommended to be secured by glue or tacky hair spray or even tape. Lace glue yields the most visually pleasing results.

Smaller, less dramatic but still very much worth the install,is the lace closure piece. It is generally much smaller than a lace frontal piece with the lace area being about 4 inches wide, 4 inches in length, but can be up to 6 inches wide, going beyond the temples. These too, come in many different lengths,textures and colors. These are smaller by far than the lace frontal,but are an easier installation. I suggest this is simpler because it really only requires needle and thread from start to finish and can look natural like it's growing out of your head,while the frontal piece needs more time and accuracy to install.

1.Can be chemically altered

2.Can take high heat

3.Versatile

4. Glueless hair pieces last longer and can be reused

5.Pieces with adhesive need to be cleaned thoroughly and reapplied anywhere from 1 to 2 weeks after install.

6.Lace closures are usually less expensive than frontals.

Kinds of Wefted Extensions

(bundles of hair on a track)

Chapter 5

Clip In Hair Extensions

Clip in extensions are another beautiful and creative way to look like you've got a fuller head of hair that can be applied in the salon or at home. Clip ins are made of human or synthetic hair. These are wefted extensions that are pre-cut.

They go inside your hair and attach to it with a clip. The back side of the clip is already sewn onto the side of the weft that will be facing your scalp.The clip is about an inch in length and has fine teeth like a comb to help secure your hair. You press the center of the clip and pop it open to slide into the area of hair you want it. Then you

can press in the center to close and secure it. These are easy to install and remove and there is no hair damage.

If your hair is fine, it's best that you tease your own hair before putting them in, so they will stay secure in your hair throughout the day. Normally, this requires only four to 5 rows of weave/wefted hair. Takes about 5-10 minutes to install and even less time to remove.

1. Human hair clip ins can be shampooed off the scalp. Just gather into the basin and shampoo thoroughly for cleaning.
2.   They are versatile.
3.   They are not permanent.
4. They can take high heat and chemicals.
5. They are interchangeable ,so you can put them back in in almost any order.

Chapter 6

Tape In Hair Extensions

Tape in Extensions are very similar to clip in extensions. They come in different colors, different lengths and every hair texture you can think of. They differ from clip extensions instead of being clipped in, they are taped in. The tape is much stronger than the typical tape found around the home and office. This type of tape is specifically meant to handle heat,humidity and last through a shampoo or two. However You can pick the strength of tapes you use if you want a more temporary install.

Tape extensions are easy to install,and they usually come pre-cut to the contour of one's head in sections from nape to fringe. You can also make these yourself.

Same as with clip extensions, the hair that is used for tepa extensions is typically human, and comes on a weft. This means the hair itself should be able to take color processing, aggressive styling and last a while.

In order to give you a detailed understanding of the installation process,imagine a sandwich. Please be sure that your hair is shampooed and free of oils. You'll take 2 wefted extensions that are already taped.Section off a thin slice of natural hair that matches the section of weft. You'll place one weft on top of the sectioned hair with the tape facing the hair, and the other hair piece on the bottom,with the tape facing the hair. There two pieces should form a sandwich so to speak and the natural hair should be enclosed inside. Run your thumb and pointer finger across both wefts on both wefts simultaneously from one end to the other to secure the hair piece in place.

Repeat until you've added your last piece near where you want it. You can also take your flat iron and home in across the wefts for a few seconds for an even better hold. Anyone with thick hair or thin hair can wear these. The key is camouflage.

1. Tape extensions can be shampooed and styles.
2. Do not damage hair.
3. Are temporary,lasting up to two weeks.
4. Very easy maintenance.
5. Last for over a year with good care.

Chapter 7

Box Braids

Box Braids are a timeless install. Dating all the way back to early egypt ,yet universally admired by all. Box braids are individual plats with a combination of one's natural hair and extension hair used to form a braid. The extension hair is usually made of synthetic fibers,called Kanekalon ,and it too comes in a variety of colors. Colors range from natural to vivid,bold and unique,along with various textures. Box braids can be styled to any length anywhere from ear length down to one's feet. They can be any thickness. In my experience box braids work better with kinky hair,in that they don't slip out right away,but they can be installed on any hair type and texture.

To begin box braids, the parts are made with a fine tooth comb and follow the bricklayer pattern. The parts form the shape of a square,c shape , zig zag or other creative methods of parting. This style takes anywhere from 4 to 10 hours to complete, and lasts up to 4 months or longer.

1.Can be shampooed.

2.Versatile styling.

3.No heat unless directed, but usually can be set in hot water.

4.Can moisturize and hydrate scalp as needed

5.Can swim in box braids without ruining hair.

Chapter 8

The Glue-in, Bond or Quickweave

Glue-in weave extensions. Glue-in extensions are attached to your hair by an adhesive. Synthetic or human hair can be used for this style. I consider it gentle, because it doesn't harden up, doesn't burn and the application is painless. It's a quick way to add length, fullness or color to your natural hair temporarily. This application lasts 2-4 weeks. It takes about an hour to apply. This style can be installed 2 ways. The extensions cut to match the portion of the head where they will be placed. The bond is then lightly spread across the inner part of the weft.

The wefts are horizontally placed directly onto the scalp from nape to fringe. The extensions can be bonded to a protective covering onto your hair,so there's slightly less long term damage to your hair.

1. This style can be flat ironed for upkeep while it lasts.

2. This style can survive gentle combing and brushing.

3. This style cannot survive shampoo.

4. Shampoo is used to help loosen and remove the adhesive bond.

Chapter 9

Traditional Braided Sew In

Another option for hair extensions sew in weave hair extensions. Sew in weave extensions can last up to 2 months depending on the method of application.

Sew-in weave extensions are sold in bundles of hair on wefts in every texture, color and length you can think of. They too, come in the human or synthetic option. Human hair ,as we said before will always outlast synthetic hair and can be reused multiple times.

Synthetic hair bundles are great as a budget friendly alternative. It still looks good, you'll just run into that tangling issue sooner.

Sew ins are installed to your hair once your hair is braided into cornrows. Pick a smooth and flat braid pattern that will not look bulky or take forever to remove. Once that's done, the weave is laid across the braids horizontally and sewn into the braids using

needle and thread for attachment and securing.Work from nape to fringe or top to bottom,and after about 2 hours you will have a finished product.

1. Can be shampooed while it's attached to your braids.
2. Styled easily.
3. Lasts 8 weeks.
4. Can be removed easily.
5. Extensions can be reused.

Make sure a skilled professional does this, to be on the safe side. The braiding is the most time consuming part of this installation. I must stress to you that it is very important to have flat and secure braids before moving forward. Usually once the braids are completed, application or weaving takes 30 minutes. Anywhere from 6 to 12 (or more) braids is a good foundation for a sew in,leaving it smooth and not taking up excessive amounts of time .

The drawback of the braided sew-in, or any extensions (just to clarify) is there may be discomfort, but it varies by the client. One client will love the way her scalp feels as it's being braided, while another may not be as appreciative.

The reason being is that your hair is meant to last, so the base and extensions must be secured so that brushing, combing, styling and shampooing doesn't remove the hair and your new style lasts several weeks.

If the hair is secured so tightly that you develop bumps, bleed, or you lose hair, it needs to be taken down and resecured, with much less tension. To be honest, I would not let someone finish my hair if the braids were too tight. It can lead to extreme discomfort and hair loss. Please

speak up for yourself. If you happen to have a sensitive scalp, please find another alternative to this installation.

Chapter 10

Braidless Sew In

The braidless sew in is one of the newer techniques to surface in popularity and can be installed in a variety of ways. This install allows you to have the appearance of a traditional sew in,but gives a person more versatility and their scalp can breath. Many people prefer this option to others.

The braidless sew in is achieved by attaching the hair weave tracks to a base other braids. Instead, the tracks are attached to micro links placed in rows horizontally throughout the scalp. Typically about 4 or 5 rows, from bottom to top.

Micro Links are tiny aluminum beads that match your hair color and are lined with silicone. The silicone inside the aluminum bead allows your hair to stay in place,once the bead is secured by clamping it closed, without damage. After this, the weave is sewn into the beads from one side to the next.

The weft is secured to the bead at each end of the track with a double knot.

1.Can be styled in many ways.

2. Will stay in your hair for up to 8 weeks.

3. Can be shampooed and styled.

4. Will need maintenance in 4 weeks to refresh the look and check the health of your own hair.

5.These extensions have been described as light as opposed to heavy while wearing.

Chapter 11

Strand by Strand Extensions

Fusion Extensions

Fusion extensions use strands of human hair,already bonded to make up a strand piece. These pieces of hair come in many lengths,textures and colors. These strand pieces are nearly the length and thickness of an average shoelace and are placed onto a small section of your natural hair 1/4 of an inch away from your scalp. On one end of these extensions is dried Keratin, or specially formulated adhesive, just for hair. Once the strands are on your hair, they are heated with a heat clamp (looks like a flat iron) for about

5-10 seconds. The application is painless and could take 2 hours or longer depending oh how many strands are being installed.

All hair extensions eventually grow out. It is best that you visit your stylist or salon every 6-8 weeks to keep your hair healthy. This is also the ideal time to have any hair extensions replaced that may have shed from natural wear.

1. Can be shampooed and styled with heat.
2. Can last a very long time.
3. Low maintenance.
4. Adds minimal volume.
5. Consultation suggested for hair shorter than 5 inches.

Chapter 12   Micro Links

Micro link extensions are similar to the fusion method in application but slightly different. The similarity is that the same kinds of hair strands are used,even though they are tipped with keratin adhesive. You also want to be sure to use the I- tip strands for easy use. The difference is that instead of using the hot tool to bind the hair extensions to the clients hair,the micro link is used. A small section of hair from your clients head is pulled downward through the micro link opening with a micro needle. Once that hair is secured through the opening, the I-tipped part of the extension strand is inserted upward through the micro link opening and placed just off the scalp. Once this happens ,you can take your set of hair pliers and apply them to the link with slight pressure and close it.

Chapter 13

Brazilian Knots

Another very popular yet time consuming installation is the Brazilian Knot technique. For this application you can use wefted hair,by cutting the wefts off of it. You can use bulk hair bundles or you can use the i-tip extensions. Similar to the micro link in that we section off a small section of hair and connect it to the extension hair. Different in the way we attach the hair to one's real hair. This method requires elastic thread. The thread should match the client's hair color. Holding the extension hair onto the hair already sectioned off, place it about ¼ inch away from the scalp. Next take the elastic thread and wrap it in a circular motion around the 2 pieces of hair to permanently attach them together.

The wrapping needs to be taut and secure so that manipulation from styling won't cause the thread to unravel. To finish off the wrapping, you want to tie both ends of the thread in a double or triple knot and clip the hanging ends away. This installation lasts a very long time.

1. Can be shampooed and blow dried.
2. Can be styled with heat.
3. Looks natural.
4. Great for volumizing hair.
5. Takes 5+ hours to install.
6. Lasts beyond 3 months with good care.

Chapter 14

Crochet Braids

Crochet braids are a quick and easy way to achieve an appearance of a lustrous voluminous head of hair without spending hours in the salon. Crochet braids come in a variety of types and textures of hair. Traditionally crochet braid hair synthetic, pre styled and doesn't require heat for maintenance. Crochet braids come in the form of bulk hair in curly,wavy crimped or straight. Crochet braids also come in traditional braid form, twists and locs. They come in natural and vivid colors, many different lengths and can be adorned by colored yarn,charms,beads or thread.

Crochet braids are installed into pre braided cornrows in the clients hair. Typically Cornrows braids are braided straight back from fringe to nape,and are connected at the ends. 6 to 12

braids,depending on the style and fullness is the average amount needed for an install. Once braids are up then the extensions are installed into the cornrows by using a regular crochet hook with a latch.Gently put the latch inside or under the braid until you see the hook appear from the other side of the cornrow. You then attach the middle piece of the strand or the looped piece of hair to the hook and close the latch.

Pull the crochet hook back towards you,and take the tail end of the hair and pull it through the loop. If the hair is pre looped, pull through no more than twice. If the hair is not pre looped, pull ends through opening,twist opening clockwise and pull ends through again. You have one finished piece. This technique must be done over and over until the cornrows are camouflaged by the extension hair. Style as desired.

1.Can be shampooed gently.

2.Easy access to the scalp to moisturize it.

3. Versatile style.

4.Does not take heat.

5.The longer it's worn,the more natural it looks.

6.Easy removal.

Chapter 15

Maintenance & Cautions

As a professional I want to remind you that even though your hair looks great for the amount of time you've worn it, you need maintenance.

1. Maintenance helps to determine the health of hair and scalp while extensions are in.
2. Seeing a professional for maintenance helps your hair and scalp to get squeaky clean.
3. Maintenance allows all adjustments to be made to make the style look new again,smell fresh and last longer.

4. Maintenance allows stylists to

communicate tips,educate you on further hair care and allows you to ask any questions you have about your install.

5. Rarely,maintenance may turn into removal if hair and scalp are irritated,inflamed or worse.

When to remove extensions

1.If you have 3 inches or more of new hair growth or re-growth.

2.If your extensions are hanging on by only a few hairs.

3.If your extensions are falling out due to excessive shampoo, chemicals or chlorine.

4.If you experience extreme scalp irritation.

5.If you experience discomfort that lasts longer than 2-4 days

6.If you experience above average hair loss noticeable hair loss.

Chapter 16

Removing extensions

Lace Bond

(for lace hair pieces)

Lace bond can be removed by applying 91% rubbing alcohol to a cotton ball or cloth and then dabbing the cloth or cotton ball onto your lace. The lace needs to be saturated so it can lift easily. This can take a few minutes. Careful not to try to separate the lace from your hairline too quickly, you could damage your skin and any surrounding hair. Once the lace is completely off, you can then use the alcohol soaked cloth to work on cleaning your skin where the lace bond was applied previously. If you have any adhesive in your hair, you can loosen it with hair oil .

You do this by applying the oil directly on top and around the area where the remaining adhesive is. Work it in and it will loosen. You can also put a shower cap on while doing this.The shower cap helps contain the heat on your head,and it helps the oil loosen the bond. You can use a fine tooth comb to remove the adhesive and go behind it with rubbing alcohol to get the sticky film off. Definitely shampoo after this.

Removing Box Braids

First ,we want to determine where to cut the braids so the natural hair is not cut. If you can detect where one's natural hair stops within the braid,then about 3 inches down from where the natural hair ends, you can cut.

You'll make 1 or 2 clean snips across the synthetic hair. Removing at this location rather than near the very ends of the braided extension piece will save time in the overall removal process. Once the braid is cut, you can use your fingers or take the end of a rat tail comb and begin to take the braid down by unraveling it so to speak. Repeat until all extension hair is removed. Detangle natural hair and shampoo.

Removing Hair Bonding Glue

(used for quickweaves)

This glue is typically black or dark grey in appearance but it can be white. It's used to bond hair extension wefts to your head quickly.

You normally find this glue on a quick weave.You can use some household products like virgin olive oil, conditioner, or just a good old shampoo to remove the weave . To get the glue out, use the same process as before, oil,shower cap and fine tooth comb. It may take some days to get the glue residue completely out.

Removing the Braided Sew In

First, you will need to locate the thread. The thread holds down the weaved or wefted hair, so it should be pretty easy. Once you locate the thread,try to slightly lift it as you cut it.This will ensure your own hair isn't accidentally cut in the process.Be very careful and take your time.

The thread matches the hair and it is very easy to cut something that belongs to you. After you cut all connected thread, the weave/wefted hair can be lifted up and removed . Once the entire weave is removed, you may begin unraveling your braid(s) with fingers or rat tail comb. Once the braid(s) are completely taken down ,then shampoo, condition and find a new style!

Removing the Braidless Sew In. Similar to the braided sew-in removal. Find thread. Lift the thread as you cut it. Cut all thread connected to the hair piece you're removing. Pull extension hair off gently. Take hair pliers and cautiously clamp the remaining flattened beads one at a time, in the opposite direction. It should be opened and look like it did before it was initially installed. Beads will slide out easily. Shampoo, etc.

Removing Fusion Extensions. This may take a while to remove .You need Acetone. It breaks up the bond of the hardened glue adhesive that attaches the extension pieces to your own hair. First, take some cotton balls, soak

in acetone,a professional brand from well known beauty retailers or a big bottle of nail polish remover will do. It's all the same. It's all acetone. Place them on the adhesive bond where your hair and the extensions meet. Wait a few seconds. If this alone does not remove the attachment,it will definitely loosen it.

Next take your hair pliers and clamp them on to the bonds,bending as you work your way to loosening that presoaked bond. Eventually the bond will break down enough to where you can remove the hair piece easily. Once all the extensions are out, you want to put oil or conditioner in hair on remaining glue pieces and with a fine tooth comb ,gently comb out. Remember to start from the ends of your hair and work upward

towards the roots.This will minimize hair breakage and it will save you some pain. Shampoo afterward.

Removing Micro Links . Take your hair pliers and apply to the aluminum beads, apply pressure onto them in the opposite way they were flattened until they open. They will slide right out. This will take only minutes. Detangle hair as needed gently ,then shampoo.

Removing Brazilian Knots

This may be the easiest to remove,but still requires you to be careful. The hair is attached by rubber thread. Take a strand connected by thread, take scissors or a razor blade and cut the know that was

created to secure the hair pieces in. Once the knot is cut, you'll need to unravel the remaining thread. If there is any resistant thread, you can cut it away in order to separate the extension hair from the natural hair. Detangle hair as needed then shampoo.

Removing Crochet Braids

Lift an individual hair piece away from the client's head. Locate the base of the crocheted piece by identifying the loop or knot. Cut the loop or knot.The cut should separate the extension piece from the cornrow. Remove by gently pulling the remainder of the extension piece out and away from the cornrow. Repeat until finished. Take the braids down by unraveling them. Detangle and shampoo. Do not cut the corn row.

Thank you for your interest in my book . I hope that this overview inspired and encouraged you, and gave you a bit of insight into the world of hair extensions. If this book was just what you were looking for,please leave a review.

−Christian Nicole

Christian Nicole's House of Beauty